W9-ATK-025

THE LITTLE GIRL WITH THE BIG VOICE

by Wé McDonald

Illustrated by
Teresa Martinez

150 East 52nd Street, Suite 32002
New York, NY 10022
www.lightswitchlearning.com

Copyright © 2018 Lightswitch Learning

All rights reserved. This book, or parts thereof, may not be reproduced in any
form or by any means, electronic, mechanical, photocopying, recording, or
otherwise, without permission in writing from the publisher, Lightswitch Learning.

Lightswitch Learning is a trademark of Sussman Education, Inc.

Educators and Librarians, for a variety of teaching resources,
visit www.lightswitchlearning.com.
Library of Congress Cataloging-in-Publication Data is available upon request.
Library of Congress Catalog Card Number pending

ISBN: 978-1-68265-585-6

The Little Girl with the Big Voice by Wé McDonald
Illustrated by Teresa Martinez
Edited by Adam Reingold
Art Direction and Book Design by Paula Jo Smith
The text of this book is set in Billy.

Printed in China

To Love, Life, and Hate,

this book is for you.

When I was a kid, I used to ride in the car with my Momma and my sister, blasting the radio, singing along as loud as we could.

3

In our house, music was everywhere. Momma was a singer, and Daddy played the drums.

Music made me come alive!

I dreamed of being a singer just like Momma. When she sang, she sounded like a beautiful bluebird—soft but strong.

But when I opened my mouth to speak, a little girl's voice came out. I sounded like a tiny, tiny squeaky mouse.

4

I would do anything to avoid speaking in class. In middle school, I was so embarrassed by my squeaky voice. I tried to keep quiet. Kids made fun of my voice. They bullied me.

Some kids even made fun of my name. "What kind of a name is Wé?" they asked. "Did your parents make it up?"

"My name is pronounced, 'way,'" I replied. "*Wé* means 'diligent' and 'committed' in an African language called Swahili."

Sometimes, I ignored the bullies.
Other times, I just walked away.

Bullying comes in many forms. It's
not always pushing and hitting someone.
Words can really hurt you, too.

My name gave me the strength and
confidence to survive each day. I was
committed to not letting people's
words hurt me. I wanted to be strong
and not give in to the bullies. Still, I
was so sad.

I tried hard to fit in. I tried pinching my nose to make it smaller.

I was too thick to fit into cool clothes. And on Dress-down Day, I never got it right.

No one wanted to be my friend. I ate lunch alone in the bathroom.

I was desperate to stop the bullying. So I tried to get my classmates to pick on someone else so they would leave me alone.

A girl named Charmaine was even quieter than I was. She didn't play with anyone. She had no friends. She just sat by herself.

"Charmaine is so weird," I said to the other kids.

10

But saying this didn't make me feel better at all. I was being just as mean as the kids who picked on me. I was being a bully. And I felt horrible! No one should pick on another person. Ever!

Charmaine was very interesting to me. She spent hours drawing beautiful patterns in her notebook.

"Can you show me how you do that?" I asked one day. She didn't say a word. She just tore out a sheet of paper and shared her colored pencils.

Soon, I started coloring with her. Finally, I had a friend.

In middle school, I didn't want to draw any attention to myself. I hoped the bullies would just leave me alone.

One day, my school had a talent show. I wanted to sing, but I didn't want to give the other kids another reason to pick on me. I was scared to participate.

Finally, I got up the courage to perform in front of the whole school. I decided to sing Alicia Keys's "Superwoman" because that was how I wanted to feel—strong and confident like a superwoman, with a big *S* on my chest.

Well, the kids at school freaked out when they heard me sing. No one expected a little girl like me to have such a deep, low singing voice.

Getting up and singing in front of the whole school, however, did not make me popular. It reminded me of what was really important: my music.

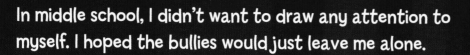

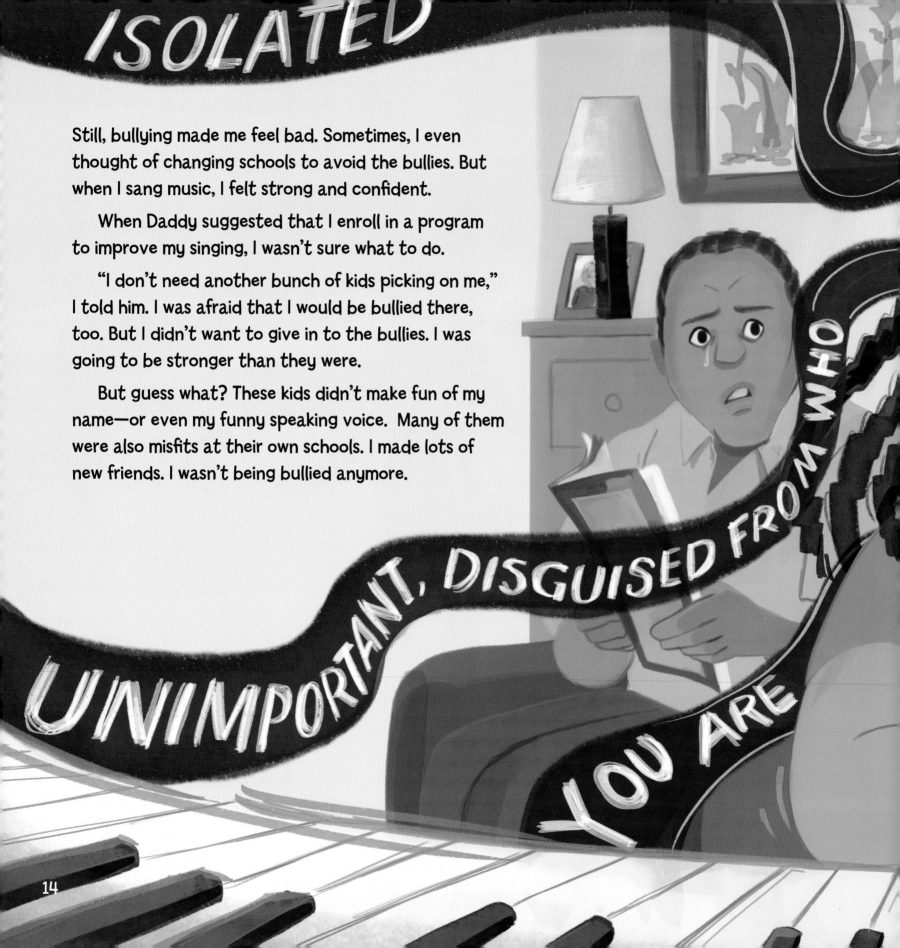

Still, bullying made me feel bad. Sometimes, I even thought of changing schools to avoid the bullies. But when I sang music, I felt strong and confident.

When Daddy suggested that I enroll in a program to improve my singing, I wasn't sure what to do.

"I don't need another bunch of kids picking on me," I told him. I was afraid that I would be bullied there, too. But I didn't want to give in to the bullies. I was going to be stronger than they were.

But guess what? These kids didn't make fun of my name—or even my funny speaking voice. Many of them were also misfits at their own schools. I made lots of new friends. I wasn't being bullied anymore.

UNIMPORTANT, DISGUISED FROM WHO YOU ARE

But I remembered what it felt like. Soon, I even started writing songs about being bullied.

Daddy heard me playing one of my songs, and he started crying.

"You have to put this out there," he said. "Your music is different."

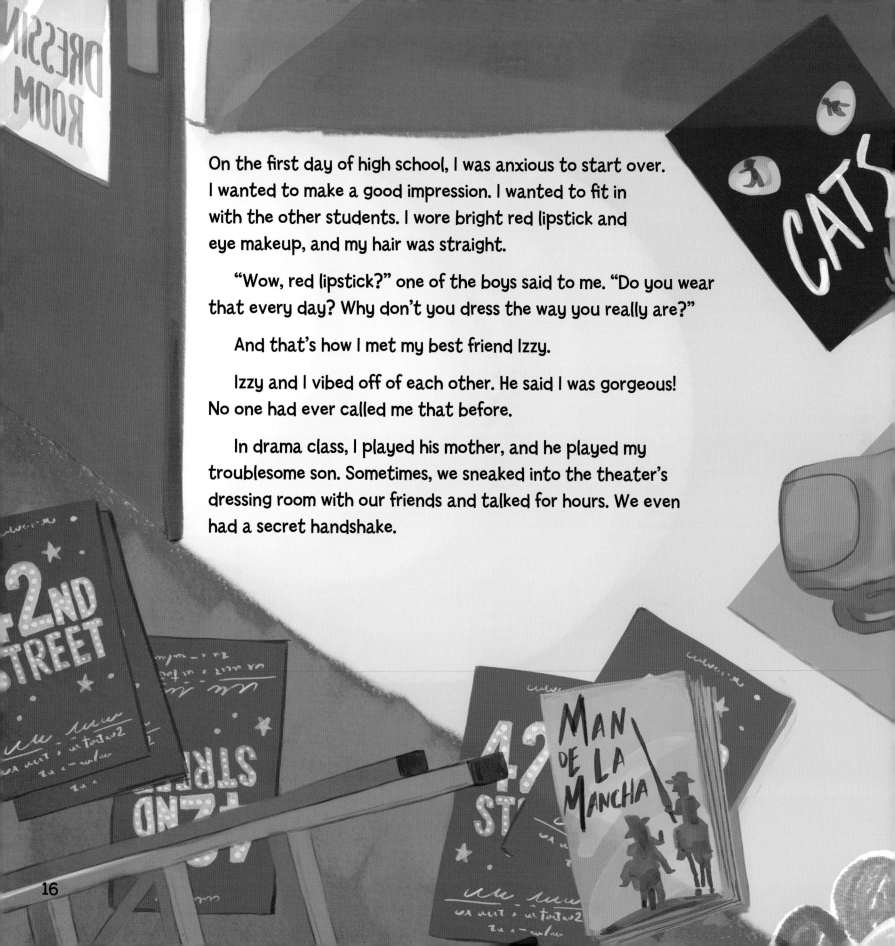

On the first day of high school, I was anxious to start over. I wanted to make a good impression. I wanted to fit in with the other students. I wore bright red lipstick and eye makeup, and my hair was straight.

"Wow, red lipstick?" one of the boys said to me. "Do you wear that every day? Why don't you dress the way you really are?"

And that's how I met my best friend Izzy.

Izzy and I vibed off of each other. He said I was gorgeous! No one had ever called me that before.

In drama class, I played his mother, and he played my troublesome son. Sometimes, we sneaked into the theater's dressing room with our friends and talked for hours. We even had a secret handshake.

I was happy being me in high school. I had many friends. I continued to improve my singing. I even found mentors like my voice teacher Miss Yolanda, who challenged me often, giving me songs performed by singers three times my age.

"I can't sing this song!" I once complained. "It's too hard." But Miss Yolanda taught me that nothing was too hard as long as you practiced.

I even got the nerve to sing at the Amateur Night at Harlem's legendary Apollo Theater. Many famous performers got their start at Apollo's Amateur Night, like Michael Jackson and the jazz singer Ella Fitzgerald.

Nobody knew who they were when they walked out on that stage for the first time.

Singing at the Apollo was the scariest moment of my life. For the first time, I was going to sing for an audience of strangers. I was only sixteen years old, so I had to compete with the grown-ups.

At the Apollo, people in the audience yell if they don't like you. They can even boo! And when they do, a man dances onstage with a broom and sweeps you off the stage!

Every seat was filled in the audience. I stood backstage nervously, waiting my turn. What if I opened my mouth and nothing came out?

Then I heard my name: "Ladies and gentleman, from Harlem, New York, here's Wé McDonald!"

As I walked on stage, I rubbed the famous tree stump for good luck. It's a superstition, but everyone does it. I planted my feet right in the middle of the stage.

Then everything went blank. I don't remember singing at all. I don't even remember seeing the audience. But I sure heard its applause! I won first place!

Now I was feeling more confident every day. I had always dreamed of being a singer—but could it actually really happen? I knew I still had to work hard to make my dream come true.

One day, Daddy did something a little crazy. He secretly sent a recording of me singing a song to the producers of the television show *The Voice*.

I was invited to audition!

There were so many people in the waiting room. Each one would stand up and sing for "practice." Some of them were just show-offs. I just sat there, watching.

They tried to coax me to sing. Daddy whispered, "Don't get up unless you have to go to the bathroom."

Guess what? None of those people made it to the show!

23

And so it happened. My biggest moment had arrived after many hours, days, and years of practice and auditions. On August 21, 2016, I waited breathlessly backstage on *The Voice*.

Millions of people were tuned in around the country to see my debut. I was so scared, I was shaking. But I couldn't chicken out. This was my dream.

What if I messed up?

24

With Alicia Keys as my coach, I felt strong.
She was like a big sister. She taught me that on
the show and in life, I didn't need to be anybody but
my true self.

Many people loved my singing. One viewer wrote online, "This
performance is divine." Another wrote, "I loved every performance."

Others started writing mean and nasty things about me after watching my videos on YouTube. Some didn't like me or my singing. They called me names and made fun of my voice! I trembled.

I was being bullied again! But this time, it was online bullying. How could people be so mean and hurtful?

I made a decision that day, and I have stuck to it. I don't read online comments anymore. It doesn't matter what other people think of me as long as I believe in myself.

Being on *The Voice* was like being in a whirlwind. It was hard work and not very glamorous.

Week after week, the competition on the show got fiercer and fiercer. I didn't know if the judges would vote for me to continue or not. But with my friends and family sitting in the audience, I knew that I was going to be okay.

Finally, months after my debut performance, the judges made their selections. Out of thousands of singers who applied, I came in third place!

Third place was good enough for me. My goal wasn't to win but to see how far I could go.

I was better than I ever thought I could be.

When I finally returned home, Izzy stood on top of his car, holding a speaker above his head. He was blasting my voice singing "Feeling Good" for everyone to hear.

Yes, finally, I had found my voice, and my dreams were coming true.

I have confidence now. Nothing can stop me. Everything is possible.

No one's voice is truly little, not even mine.

31

PRIMARY SOURCE: Song

McDonald Family Archive

Primary sources like a song provide a window into the thoughts of people. Writing songs and performing them help me express my feelings and share them with people around the world.

As humans, we are beautiful and powerful people. We all have deep feelings and emotions that are meaningful to us. I like to write and perform songs so that I can express my feelings and share them with people around the world.

Today, I continue to build my singing career around the world. I am so excited to share my song "Head Up High" with others. I wrote this song to inspire all of us to never give up, to always believe in ourselves.

This is the first time I have shared this song with others. I am excited to announce that this song will be included in my first EP to be released shortly.

Head Up High

By Wé McDonald
and Kylie Rothfield

Darling I'm holding my head up high.
I know my dreams will touch the sky.
Darling I'm holding my head up high.

Other people think they know me.
Other people judge what they see.
There's a voice inside that keeps me going on.

Darling I'm holding my head up high.
I know my dreams will touch the sky.
And oh, and I know and I know,
Darling I'm holding my head up high.

Broke back...
Big heart, with a thick skin...
Strong mind...
Big hair, like my mom did
Taught me, brought me...
From a bad place of mind...
I'm fed up
With the expectation.
Too thick, lose weight...
Then you're too thin.
Teach me, bring me
From a bad place of mind.

And other people swear they know me.
Other people judge what they see.
There's a voice inside that keeps me
Going on.

Darling I'm holding my head up high.
I know my dreams will touch the sky.
And oh, and I know and I know,
Darling I'm holding my head up high.
A million voices shattering the ceiling
Come together through the heartache and
the healing.
A million problems breaking through the concrete...
We are the roses with blood on the leaves.
A million voices shattering the ceiling
Come together through the heartache and
the healing.
A million problems breaking through the concrete...
We are the roses with blood on the leaves.

I'm holding my head up high.
I know my dreams will touch the sky.
And oh, and I know and I know,
Darling I'm holding my head up high.

I'm holding my head up high.
I know my dreams will touch the sky.
And oh, and I know and I know,
Darling I'm holding my head up high.

Holding...
Got me holding my head up...
Holding...
Got me holding my head up...
Holding...
Got me holding my head up...
Holding...
Got me holding my head up high...

DEPTH OF KNOWLEDGE

Discussion Questions

1. Why did Wé want to become a singer?

2. According to the author, when Wé's mother sang, she sounded like a "beautiful bluebird." When Wé spoke, she sounded like a "tiny, tiny squeaky mouse." What does the author mean by this? How are these descriptions alike? How are they different?

3. Have you ever been nervous or anxious about something? How did you overcome your anxiety?

4. According to the author, bullying comes in many forms. What kinds of bullying have you seen? What's one thing you could do if you see someone being bullied?

5. Is there anyone in school or at home to whom you could talk if you were bullied, or if you saw that someone else was being bullied? Explain.

6. Describe the different ways that bullying is hurtful to others. What did Wé do to overcome being bullied?

7. In high school, Wé practiced for many hours to improve her singing. Give an example of a time when you achieved something after working hard. Describe how it felt.

8. What are three things you can do to overcome challenges in order to meet your goals in life?

9. Why did you think Wé's father secretly sent a recording of her singing to *The Voice*?

10. What does the author mean on page 31 when she says, "No one's voice is truly little"?

Activities

1. Write a poem about an activity, sport, or hobby you enjoy. Share it with the class.

2. Draw a picture that shows how a person might feel when he or she is bullied.

3. Read the words to Wé's song on page 33. Explain why you think her words will or will not inspire others to never give up when they are faced with great challenges.

4. Create a poster listing the skills that are important for people who want to meet their goals. Include a description of how each of these skills helps a person to reach his or her goals.

5. Choose a person with a successful career in your community whom you would like to interview. Create a news report featuring your interview.

Group Activity

Understand and manage anxiety

Write a song that can help others to manage their anxiety.

Work in groups:

- Think about a time when you were nervous or anxious.

- Research different things that people can do to feel less anxious.

- Discuss how you handled anxiety in the past and how you will handle it if it happens again.

- Write a song that explains how to reduce anxiety. See page 33 for an example of words in a song.

- Share each song with the class.

GLOSSARY

Amateur *(noun)* someone who takes part in a hobby or activity for fun and not for pay *(p. 18)*

Anxious *(adjective)* being worried or stressed out *(p. 16)*

Backstage *(noun)* an area behind a stage *(p. 20)*

Breathlessly *(adverb)* nervously *(p. 24)*

Bullied *(verb)* to have frightened, hurt, or threatened someone *(p. 6)*

Coax *(verb)* to talk someone into doing something *(p. 23)*

Committed *(adjective)* dedicated and loyal *(p. 6)*

Competition *(noun)* a contest between people *(p. 28)*

Confidence *(noun)* a feeling that you can do something well *(p. 7)*

Courage *(noun)* being strong and brave even though you might be frightened *(p. 12)*

Debut *(noun)* a person's first performance *(p. 24)*

Desperate *(adjective)* being beyond hope *(p. 10)*

Diligent *(adjective)* working hard and with great care *(p. 6)*

Disguised *(adjective)* the changed appearance of something in order to hide its true look *(p. 14)*

Divine *(adjective)* excellent *(p. 26)*

Dressing room *(noun)* a place where performers change clothes before a show *(p. 16)*

Fierce *(adjective)* intense and powerful *(p. 28)*

Glamorous *(adjective)* exciting and attractive *(p. 28)*

Impression *(noun)* a thought or opinion of something *(p. 16)*

Isolated *(adjective)* set apart from others *(p. 14)*

Legendary *(adjective)* very famous and well respected *(p. 18)*

Mentor *(noun)* a trusted teacher or advisor *(p. 18)*

Misfit *(noun)* someone who has a hard time fitting in *(p. 14)*

Participate *(verb)* to take part and join in something *(p. 12)*

Pattern *(noun)* a series of lines *(p. 11)*

Producer *(noun)* a person in charge of making a TV show or movie *(p. 22)*

Program *(noun)* a planned activity *(p. 14)*

Pronounced *(verb)* to have said a word out loud *(p. 6)*

Selection *(noun)* someone or something that has been chosen *(p. 29)*

Superstition *(noun)* a belief in something that cannot be proven *(p. 20)*

Talent *(noun)* a special skill *(p.12)*

Tree stump *(noun)* the bottom part of a tree left over after the tree has been cut down *(p. 20)*

Trembled *(verb)* shook due to fear or worry *(p. 27)*

Troublesome *(adjective)* to cause trouble *(p.16)*

Vibed *(verb)* to have given off an emotion or feeling to another person *(p. 16)*

Whirlwind *(noun)* a confused rush of emotion *(p. 28)*

Acknowledgments

To my parents and Jazzy: You guys stood by my side, before anyone did, through everything, and I can't thank you enough for that. You instilled creativity, love, passion, morals, and compassion in me. This is a product that you've helped mold. I couldn't do this without you. I LOVE YOU!

To my sisters: Thank you for the protection that you've always given me. Sisters forever!

To Ron and Steve Sussman: This book could not have happened without you and your beautiful mind-set. This is more than just my book; it's yours as well.

To Adam Reingold: The previous message applies to you, too! This was something you devoted your time and effort into. You organized everything and kept us all insane and sane all at the same time— Thank you!

To Teresa Martinez: You captured my life and put it on paper perfectly. The way you illustrated the emotions and body movements with color and vibrancy was insane! You were the perfect illustrator.

To Ann Lewinson: Girl, you've heard me talk longer than my parents have heard me talk. You listened and transcribed beautifully. You made my life seem more magical than ever. Thank you for also knowing my crazy family. We really appreciate the work you've done.

To My Best Friends: I'm sorry if all of you guys aren't in the book. You know I love you and I would show you off in a second! Think of it as one of Mr. Smith's plays and you didn't make the cut, but stage crew is always another option. Listen, don't think that just because you're in stage crew, you don't still have to "BE OFF BOOK YESTERDAY!" Much love.

To my mentors: I wasn't easy to deal with nor will I ever be, but that's the fun part. Thank you for kicking me in the butt when I needed it and then comforting me after it left a bruise. There were times that made me want to give up, but you guys were always there to tell me not to. This is part of the outcome of what YOU did. Congratulations!

To My Little Noah: Keep being free, Nunu. I love you with all of my heart. I'll give you all the kisses and mugamugas there ever were. I'm so proud of you, and when you learn to read this, you better start crying!